Hidden Harbours of Southwest Britain

Published by
Imray Laurie Norie & Wilson Ltd
Wych House St Ives
Cambridgeshire PE27 5BT England
☎ +44 (0)1480 462114
Fax +44 (0)1480 496109
Email ilnw@imray.com
www.imray.com
2010

978 184623 204 6

British Library Cataloguing in Publication Data.
A catalogue record for this title is available from the British Library.

Printed in Singapore by Star Standard Industries Pte

Hidden Harbours

OF SOUTHWEST BRITAIN

Dag Pike

IMRAY LAURIE NORIE & WILSON

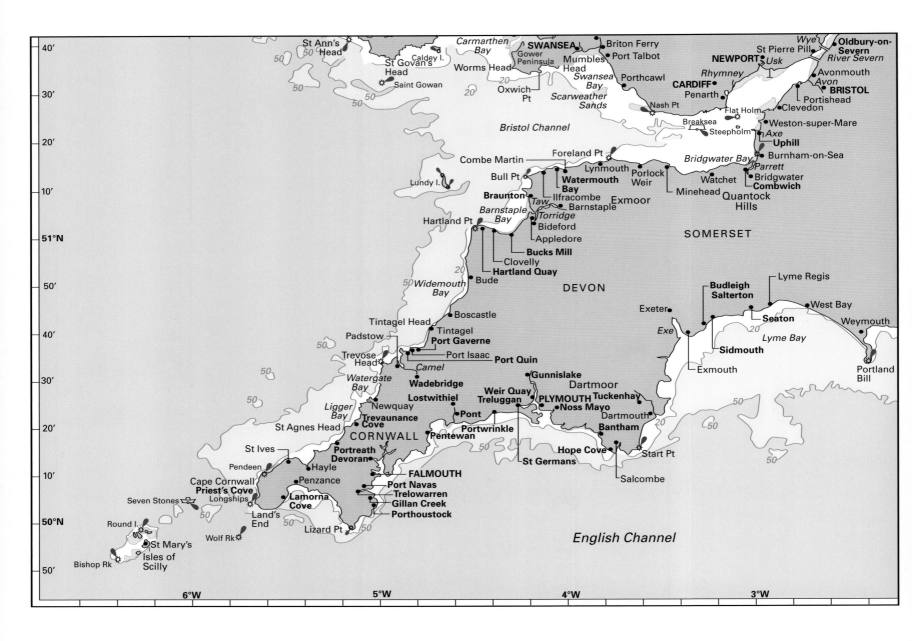

Contents

Introduction

It is not easy to find a definition of a hidden harbour. Each harbour in this book has its own definition, partly depending on history, partly depending on its current status and use and partly depending on how interesting it might be for a visitor. What was intriguing in researching this book was just how many hidden harbours there are around the coast. Some have fallen into disuse and are hardly recognisable as harbours anymore and have almost disappeared off the map, some have changed their use from commercial to leisure craft whilst others have a very different function to that for which they were originally constructed, perhaps being originally developed as fishing ports and now focusing on the tourist trade. What is apparent is that they all have a rich history where they may have been developed and then declined only to rise again or where they may be slowing sliding into oblivion. Some have been preserved for future generations and some were once amongst the major ports of Britain whilst others have played only a minor part in the commerce of the country.

Many of these hidden harbours in southwest Britain can trace their origins to the Roman invasion. The Romans arrived by boat and did much of their exploration of the country by boat establishing harbours as they went. The Romans were after the minerals such as lead, silver and antimony that were found, particularly in Cornwall but today there are very few traces of the Roman influence any longer and fishing and trade became the main reason for ports to exist. The demand for port facilities grew rapidly in the 17th and 18th centuries when coal took over from wood as a main source of fuel and products such as farm produce, bricks and minerals started to move around the country but it was primarily the mineral exploitation in Cornwall that was responsible for much of the port development.

At the time road transport was still in the horse and cart era and the railways had not been invented so the transport of anything that was heavy or bulky had to go by water if possible. To reduce the overland journey to a minimum ports were established as close to the mines and quarries as possible and it was this that lead to the development and building of what today are many of the hidden harbours featured in this book. Some of these harbours, particularly those on the north coast of Devon and Cornwall were built in what would now be considered to be impossible situations, having little regard to the strength and violence of the sea. This optimism that man could challenge the might of the Atlantic storms demonstrates how important it was to establish harbours as close to the source of mines and quarries as possible and even when harbours were washed away in a storm they were often rebuilt again and again.

Lostwithiel, once the major port in Cornwall and now a little backwater

When the Romans came to the West Country for the minerals they only touched the surface and exploration in the 17th and 18th centuries found rich deposits that were ready for exploitation by a country starting its Industrial Revolution. Whilst the minerals were being shipped out, mainly to South Wales where there was abundant coal for the smelting operations there was a two way trade with coal coming in to provide the steam power required for the mine pumps and embryo steam powered mineral railways.

However, even before steam power was in use coal was required for the limekilns that were to become a feature of many of the ports of the southwest. Limekilns were built to 'burn' the raw limestone that was either imported or quarried out of the hills and coal was required for this burning process. The limestone would be alternated with layers of coal in the limekiln and left to burn for two or three days, the 'burning' process turning the limestone into lime. Lime was used in three ways, as the basis of mortar in building work, as a lime wash for painting houses and for spreading on the land to counter acidic soils. The last was important on the low-lying fields of the Somerset levels but it was also used on the soils of West Cornwall.

For years there was two way trade across the Bristol Channel, minerals and lime going out and coal coming in. It sounds an easy trade route but the Bristol Channel is one of the wildest stretches of water around the British coastline, wide open to the Atlantic and having some of the strongest tides in the world. The rise and fall of the tide is also exceptional, and this allowed rivers and creeks that were just expanses of mud or rock at low water to become viable ports as the tide rose. For the ports on the south coasts of Devon and Cornwall there was the challenging voyage around Lands End to add to the dangers of the voyage.

The entrance to Uphill which would have challenged the seamanship skills of the mariners

The sailors who navigated these waters had to be exceptional seamen, able to cope with the challenging sea and weather of the Bristol Channel and capable of feeling their way up narrow twisting channels using only wind power and perhaps assisted by oars. In many of the harbours just getting into a narrow entrance from the stormy seas outside could be a challenge and remember there were no weather forecasts in those days. There was none of the pressure of time that exists with modern shipping and if it took a couple of tides to get into harbour nobody was complaining but at every turn these seaman were at the mercy of the weather and

The Longships Lighthouse off Lands End where there are rocks that were a threat to the early navigators

Lands End, the major turning point on a voyage from the English Channel into the Bristol Channel

there were few places on these coasts to run and hide form the storms.

The ships and boats used for this trade were tiny by modern standards. A 100-footer would be a large vessel and many were smaller to cope with the very limited facilities and shallow waters in many of these small harbours. Cargoes were shipped out in small batches, often loaded and discharged by baskets on men's shoulders. Shore facilities might comprise a hand operated crane but mostly the ships's gear would be used for loading and discharge. A horse and cart might come alongside when the ship dried out at low water so that cargo could be loaded directly into the cart. Handling the cargoes was a

very physical activity but in many of the ports there were some very ingenious loading systems developed that would at least allow the loading to be done by gravity.

The south coast ports operated differently to those on the north coast. Many of these ports were used for exporting minerals and importing coal but this meant that the ships involved in this trade had to negotiate the wild seas around Land's End. This could be a challenge to the best of seamen with the waves powering in from the Atlantic and the ships have to negotiate what would often be a lee shore where any mistake or misjudgement could mean the ship ending up on the rocks.

So whilst there was coal and mineral trade, many of the south coast ports turned to their southern neighbour France for trade and there was a flourishing wine trade both legal and illegal. The south coasts of Devon and Cornwall are well endowed with good harbours, both those on the sunken river valleys such as Falmouth, Fowey, Plymouth and Exeter, and the many smaller ports with man-made breakwaters. The big ports were the trading ports and most of the smaller ports focussed on fishing with the illegal smuggling trade being focused more on smaller ports where the smugglers thought they could escape the Revenue.

Along both coastlines of southwest Britain it is always surprising how ports were created and used in the past but you have to remember that carrying goods by sea was both the cheapest and the most practical means of transport. Road transport of anything bulky or heavy was virtually impossible given the state of the roads and it was only when the railway came to the southwest that things changed. The railways provided a viable and safer alternative to shipping and the ports and their ships struggled to compete. Then sailing ships were replaced by steam ships and the balance swung back in favour of shipping again but steamships worked in conjunction with the railways so that the ships tended to use only the larger and more established ports.

By the beginning of the 20th century many of the smaller harbours fell into decline, as their trade was swallowed by ports that could offer easy and safe access to larger ships. Many of these smaller ports became the hidden harbours of this book, still there but rarely used and without funds to provide dredging or improved facilities. Many found their salvation in the booming leisure sailing business and this is what keeps many of these small ports and harbours going these days. Where there used to be trading schooners you now find sailing and power yachts, the quality of the harbour facilities usually dictating the quality of the yachts using them.

Hidden Harbours looks at the history of many of these small harbours around the coast and relates their current condition. They can make an interesting alternative for visiting yachtsmen looking for somewhere off the beaten track to visit and explore perhaps by small tenders. They can be of interest to the land visitor looking to trace the industrial archaeology of harbours and the reasons for its rise and decline. They can be of interest to the walker along the Coastal Paths who can compare the history of a place with its present state.

Hidden Harbours of Southwest Britain aims to paint a picture of what harbours were like in the past and what they are like now. These harbours may be outside the normal run of visitor attractions and it is surprising how many places have turned their backs on the harbours that were the reason for their creation and are now seeking their fortune from tourists flocking to nearby beaches. However many of the harbours were built to last and they can be rich in history and rewarding to visit both by land and sea.

Trevaunance Cove where the once busy harbour is now just a pile of stones

Seaton, Lyme Bay

Seaton was at the end of the Fosse Way so is likely to have been a port in Roman times. At one time ships were going up the River Axe as far as Musbury and Colyford but silting and reclamation reduced the tidal flow needed to keep the river clear so that the shingle bank at the entrance started to build up. In the Middle Ages a pier was built at the entrance to try and keep the channel clear and ships of up to 150 tons could use the port. However, by 1537 the port was only available to fishing boats after a landslip on the cliffs had narrowed the entrance. Whilst the main port was at Seaton at the entrance ships would head up river to Axmouth as well.

A larger pier was built at the entrance in 1803 and this opened up the harbour again but it was destroyed on 1869. Around this time the railway came to Seaton and the lower bridge was built reducing the need for and the scope for the harbour and it went into decline from then on. This lower bridge built in 1877 is the oldest standing concrete

The main quay at Seaton now used mainly by angling boats

bridge in Britain but it was closed to traffic in 1990 when the new bridge just up river was built. The tourist trade developed and the harbour returned to the fishermen who are the only commercial users today and most of them are angling boats. The entrance has been stabilised to a large degree by a new pier and training wall that helps to scour the channel although the shingle bank on the west side is still mobile after storms and constantly threatens to narrow down the entrance.

Access by road

The A358 from Chard leads to a cross roads outside Colyford and then the B3172 leads to Axmouth and on to Seaton. The road to the east side of the harbour turns off left just before the bridge but there is no parking here and the next left over the bridge is the best solution.

Parking

Pay and display on the sea front and some street parking.

Water access

Yachts and fishing boats regularly use the harbour but local knowledge helps a lot. Head up for the beacon on the east pier heading 030°T and then hug close to the jetty as it swings round to the NNW and the harbour opens up. There is a very strong tide in the entrance so around high water is the best time to enter when the tide slackens off.

Facilities

Seaton has most of the facilities of a small town. There is a café on the quay on the east side of the harbour and two pubs, a bistro and a store on the west side. The Axe Yacht Club welcomes visitors and there is a small marina on the east side of the harbour with visitors' moorings.

More information

www.axeyachtclub.co.uk
www.seatonbay.com

Comments

Seaton is a magical place combining the requirements of yachtsmen, fishermen and holiday makers without apparent confliction. The entrance channel running under the cliffs makes for spectacular views and a trip up river by dinghy is rewarding. The harbour entrance appears to have been stabilised, at least until the next big storm when history may repeat itself.

The shingle bank on the west side of the entrance tries to close off the channel after storms

The narrow entrance channel at Seaton where the strong tide helps to keep the channel clear

Sidmouth, Lyme Bay

Sidmouth is the harbour that has tried to make the big time on several occasions but has never quite got there. In the 15th and 16th centuries the harbour established on the narrow River Sid was reported as one of the important fishing towns of Devon and ships from Sidmouth were engaged in the Newfoundland cod fishing. However the great storm of 1824 washed away protection from the Chit Rock ledge to the west of the town and allowed silt to build up across the river entrance.

It was partly this and partly the work on building the wall along the sea front that led to proposals for a major harbour construction comprising two stone piers extending out from the area south of the town. Work actually started in 1837 with the building of the initial inshore ends of the piers and a railway was constructed along the sea front to bring in stone

The training jetty and the slipway that are the only facilities at Sidmouth today

from the coast to the east but then work stopped and was never started again. History repeated itself as recently as 2007 when there were proposals for a marina to be built extending out from the sea front but nothing has started.

The original harbour along the River Sid was very narrow but the remains of wharves can be seen today. The width of the river meant that it would never be a major port as it limited the size of ships that could use it and today the local fishing fleet operates from the beach, with protection from a short stone pier extending out from the west side of the river entrance. The original river port is just a narrow stretch of river almost hidden from view.

Access by road

From the A3052 road take the B3175 into the town. The river and harbour lie to the east of the main part of the town.

Parking

There is limited street parking in the town and along the sea front and a small pay and display car park behind the sailing club.

Water access

The river harbour is not accessible but it is possible to anchor off and land on the shingle beach by the fishing boats. Beware of an outfall pipe that runs out to seaward with the end marked by a yellow buoy.

Facilities

There are all the facilities of a small town at Sidmouth including pubs, hotels and cafés. The Sidmouth Sailing and Sea Angling Club is adjacent to the river mouth and the inshore lifeboat station is alongside it.

More information

www.sidmouth.ws

Comments

When you see the narrow river at Sidmouth today it is hard to believe that it was once a busy fishing harbour, but the eastward drift of the shingle along this coast has provided a constant struggle to keep the harbour entrance accessible. This river is now controlled by weirs that reduce the flushing effect of the river flow. The footbridge over the entrance to the river was built in 1855 from timbers taken from a ship wrecked on the beach.

The entrance has been completely silted up by the shingle bank

The remains of the narrow harbour that was once busy with ships

Budleigh Salterton, Lyme Bay

The name of Budleigh Salterton comes from the salt pans that were established in the estuary by the monks of nearby Otterton Priory. These were large enclosed shallow areas where saltwater was left to evaporate to extract the valuable salt. The harbour has had a chequered career and it was once an open estuary but always suffered from the shingle spits that tended to be thrown up after major storms. It is thought that the present shingle spit originated from the Great Storm of 1824 and today it almost completely blocks off the river entrance, leaving just a narrow channel through which the tide pours. East Budleigh further up the River Otter was a small port in the 12th and 13th centuries and boats travelled up as far as Otterton where the bridge crossing of the river was established.

The town itself, which lies to the west of the river, was an important fishing port in the past but with the boats launching off the open beach rather than using the river.

In 1810 the entrance channel was navigable by 60 ton vessels and there are the remains of limekilns built into the west side of what is now a large car park. It is reported that flat-bottomed boats brought the limestone across from Brixham whilst coal would be brought round from South Wales. Exports would have been mainly agricultural produce but the harbour was never on the main trade routes because of its difficult entrance and narrow winding channels. Today the River Otter channels have been given over largely as a bird sanctuary although it is still possible to see the remains of the channels that were cut in the reed beds to give access to small wharves.

rocks

An artificial channel that was cut through the marshes to reach the old quay in the foreground

Access by road

From Exmouth take the B3178 to the east and from the west the same road turns off the A3052 at Newton Poppleford. Budleigh Salterton is well signposted but for the harbour you need to head to the east side of town.

Parking

There is a large pay and display car park on the east side of town close by the river and right alongside the estuary and shingle bank.

Water access

It would be possible to enter the River Otter at high water but the entrance is now very narrow and overhung by the undercut cliffs on the east side and with the strong currents it could be dangerous. Boats are discouraged because the area is now a bird sanctuary. It is possible to anchor off in settled conditions but beware of the Otterton Ledge that extends out 400 yards from the entrance.

Facilities

Budleigh Salterton has all the facilities of a small town and there is a kiosk in the car park for snacks.

More information

www.budleighsalterton.org

Comments

Budleigh Salterton grew from a small fishing port into a Victorian holiday resort when the railway came to the town. The town has now become gentrified and is full of retirement homes and the sense of history has been almost obliterated from the area around the River Otter in the name of conservation. There are still the remains of the limekiln near the car park but they have been incorporated into a low wall and there is virtually no trace of the harbour. However, the shingle bank and the narrow entrance are well worth a visit, giving a fascinating insight into the way storms and tides have shaped and virtually destroyed this harbour.

The very narrow entrance channel is dominated by the cliff on the undercut cliff on the east side

The remains of the old limekilns

Tuckenhay, River Dart

Tuckenhay is located up a creek that heads west off the River Dart. Dartmouth, Kingswear and Totnes were the major ports on the Dart so Tuckenhay was always in the second league, with the sea traffic heading up Bow Creek to Tuckenhay serving the needs of the local community rather than a wider market. Ships and barges have traded on the creek for hundreds of years, bringing in coal and limestone for the limekilns on the quays and cereals for the brewing industry that flourished on the creek. The remains of limekilns can be seen along the main road into the village and built into the surroundings of the Maltsters Arms pub. Cider was made on the creek and both drunk locally and exported and because of its hidden nature Tuckenhay is reputed to have been a favourite haunt of smugglers.

The river at Tuckenhay creek has a number of old quays

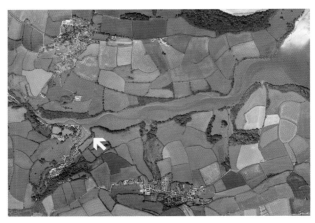

Tuckenhay Mill up a narrow arm off the main creek was noted as a manufacturer of fine paper that was used for bank notes and royal proclamations. The mill has now closed and has been converted into time share apartments and cottages. In addition to its fame as the home of this unique paper mill, Tuckenhay is reputed to have had the first gas street lighting although strangely there is now no street lighting in the village at all.

The last ship to bring cargo to the creek was in 1939 and today the only traffic is visiting yachts.

Access by road

The easiest route is from the Dartmouth road, the A 3122 where a right turn near Drevton Cross picks up the road to Cornworthy and then Tuckenhay. Alternatively take the Ashprington road out of Totnes and take the turning to Bow and then Tuckenhay. Postcode for the satnav is TQ9 7EH.

Parking

Very little along the road but the pub car park is spacious and available provided you use the pub.

Water access

Follow the winding channel up the creek from the River Dart. This runs roughly in the centre of the creek and is marked by pole beacons. Yachts can tie up at the Maltsters Arms and even stay there overnight by prior arrangement although the berth dries out.

Facilities

The Maltsters Arms offers both meals and accommodation as well as drinks.

More information

www.tuckenhay.com

Comments

Whilst Tuckenhay has changed completely from a busy bustling small working harbour into a hidden away tourist village it is still a fascinating place. Many of the houses along the river bank prevent water access but the pub has no such restrictions and so will be the focus for the visitor both by land and sea. Many of the names of the houses are prefixed with Old such as Old Quay House, Old Bakery, Old Mill House demonstrating how much the character of the village has changed but it is still worth the visit.

The remains of the old limekilns on the road into Tuckenhay

The quay at the Maltsters Arms where yachtsmen are welcomed

Hope Cove, Bigbury Bay

As far as legitimate activities go Hope Cove has largely been a fishing village with local boats roaming out from the cove into the English Channel. Its tidal restrictions, rock strewn entrance and exposure to winds from the west and southwest meant that it was never going to hit the big time, and tucked away behind Bolt Tail it was not a convenient harbour for cargo. Its remote location meant that it was a great place for smuggling and there seems little doubt that the fishing was the respectable cover for the illegal activities. The harbour was developed by linking some of the outlying rocks to the west of the beach to create a breakwater that offers some protection from the westerly gales but swell coming into the beach of the harbour would still restrict activities.

Access by road

The turning for Hope Cove is off the main road between Kingsbridge and Salcombe, the A361. Take the turning on the right sign-posted to Galumpton and Outer Hope and head down to the beach and harbour at the bottom of the hill. The road carries on to Inner Hope where the lifeboat station was located further round the cove. Postcode for satnav TQ7 3HQ.

The old lifeboat house tucked into the corner of Hope Cove

Parking

There is a paying car park just as the road arrives at the first beach but it is quite small. Hotels and pubs have their own parking if you plan to visit them and there are a few short term parking spaces near the harbour.

Water access

Bolt Tail is the distinctive headland that guides the way in from seaward and can be passed close to. Once round the headland the village and the breakwater become visible and the main rock to watch for is Goody Rock. A bearing of ESE to the old lifeboat house gives a clear run in but watch for mooring buoys in the summer. Overnight anchorage is possible in settled weather or when the wind is

The harbourmaster at Hope Cove does love his notices to control visitors

from anywhere in the east and there is landing in the harbour on the beach or alongside the breakwater but watch for rocks off the end of the breakwater and to the south. Boats can be launched from the harbour beach for a fee. There is no large scale chart of the area.

Facilities

There are good facilities at Hope Cove, the Hope and Anchor pub, the Cove, the Sun Bay and the Cottage Hotels, a café plus the post office/stores and a few souvenir shops. A private inshore rescue boat is based at Hope Cove.

More information

Harbourmaster ☎ 01548 560 928.

Comments

Hope Cove is a rarity in that it is largely unspoilt around the harbour with thatched cottages and small houses huddling together. The new development is nearly all above the village. The remoteness of Hope Cove has meant that it tends to guard its privacy but this is a place well worth a visit for its beaches, for its scenery and for its good facilities.

Hope Cove at low tide showing the breakwater that offers some protection from westerly gales

Bantham, Bigbury Bay

A decorative alcove on the thatched harbourmaster's building

The harbourmaster's building on the quay at Bantham

Bantham has always been in the minor league of harbours because of the difficult entrance to the River Avon on which it stands. This means that it remained a small coastal and fishing port mainly serving just the local countryside. It would accommodate mainly shallow draft coastal schooners and cargoes were trans-shipped at Bantham for onward movement some four miles up river to Aveton Gifford by barge. Like all the small ports on the South coasts fishing was important and the pilchard fishing relics can be seen in the names of small quays called Upper and Lower cellars where the pilchards were processed and stored before onward transit.

Access by road

Single track roads for about 4 miles from the roundabout on the A381 just south of Aveton Gifford. A postcode of TQ7 3AN in the satnav will lead to the village.

Parking

A car park run by the Evans Estates is virtually the only parking in the village and they only offer a daily rate and no short term parking. If you want access to the sea beach then you have to pay this parking.

Water access

The entrance is wide open to the SW and so is only easily negotiable in settled weather or Easterly winds. It is best entered on the flood near high water leaving conspicuous Burgh Island and the beacon marking off-lying rocks to the north. The channel tends to follow the outside of the curves in the river. Once inside most of the river is occupied by moorings so contact the harbourmaster for advice. The river up to Aveton Gifford is worth exploring by dinghy.

Facilities

The Bantham Sailing Club appears to protect its privacy by not offering contact details or a telephone number. The Sloop Inn in the village is a great pub that also offers accommodation and there is a village stores.

More information

Harbourmaster ☎ 01548 561196.

Comments

Bantham and the River Avon are virtually unspoilt and very beautiful. A thatched building on the quay below the village is the harbourmaster's base and has figureheads on the walls. Further down river on the south bank there are Jenkin's Quay and the Upper and Lower Cellars Quays but road access to all of them is difficult. Dinghy racing takes place in the river in the summer.

The River Avon at Bantham where the remains of an old low water quay can be seen

Noss Mayo, River Yealm

The old wharf at Bridgend Quay

A view down the pill at Noss Mayo

The strange name of this village comes from Noss meaning promontory which was owned by Mathew (Mayo). The region was dominated by Newton Ferrers on the opposite bank and this has enabled Noss Mayo to retain much of its historical charm and features although modern development is starting to change this. In the past Noss Mayo was largely a fishing village, which is surprising considering its distance from the sea. It is thought that many of the old waterfront buildings started life as fish cellars for use when the pilchard fishing was at its height.

There is little trace of these cellars left now although some of the old wharves such as Bridgend Quay can still be seen. This quay is now used as a boat park but it was once the place where sailing coastal ships would bring in cargoes of coal, limestone and other cargoes and taking out mainly farm produce and fish. In the early 19th century a ferry service linked the area to Plymouth but as this had to go out into the open waters of the Channel this must have been very much at the mercy of the weather.

Access by road

From the A370 at Yealmton take the A3186 that is signed to Newton Ferrers. Before entering that village take a left turn to Bridgend and then on to Noss Mayo. The postcode for the satnav is PL8 1EW.

Parking

In the village itself parking is impossible with the very narrow streets but there is parking on the hard at Bridgend Boat Park and further into the village on the creek itself just before the Ship Inn down a turning to the right. This parking is very limited near high water.

Water access

Past the Great Mewstone the leading beacons should show up to provide a guide into the narrow entrance close into the south side. From there a second set of

leading beacons leads into the River Yealm where the river is crowded with moorings. The Newton Ferrers arm is off to the right with the Noss Mayo Pill a further turning to the right about half a mile up the Arm. Beware of a raised stone walkway across the Pill linking the two pubs, which is about 4 feet above the bed of the Pill.

Facilities

The Ship Inn and the Swan lie on opposite sides of the Pill and are linked by a walkway which can be used when it surfaces near low water. Both pubs have a landing stage available from about half tide onwards. The village has all the usual facilities and there is a launch slip for small craft in the harbour.

More information

Harbourmaster ☏ 01752 872533
Yealm Yacht Club ☏ 01752 872291
www.yealmyachtclub.co.uk

Comments

The entrance to the River Yealm is exposed to the southwest but it has deeper water than nearby river entrances and so is much more popular. In consequence the river banks are more densely populated and the river itself more crowded with boats. However, it is still very beautiful and despite

the housing development along the banks the area still feels very unspoilt. The village of Noss Mayo still has a traditional feel and there has been little attempt at new development although the use of the buildings has changed to residential rather than commercial use. There are miles of unspoilt river upstream to explore by dinghy and for walkers there are some great riverside walks.

The raised stone walkway across the pill linking the two pubs at low water

Weir Quay, River Tamar

Weir Quay is one of the many small harbours and quays that lined the banks of the River Tamar above Plymouth. These quays were built to import coal and timber for the mines and limestone for the farms and for building as well as exporting the ore from the mines. Weir Quay is one of the first of these quays above Plymouth and lies just before a sharp U-turn in the river channel and so it benefits from the deep water on the outside of the bend. Some of these quays such as Cothele have been restored to near original condition but Weir Quay has the deserted and desolate look of having been abandoned once the mine trade stopped.

Limekilns behind the quay speak of the inbound trade and like most of the quays coal and timber for the mines were the main imports with the mined ore being the main export. To take the coal up and to bring the ore down there was an inclined tramway built up the hillside and the track of this can still be seen. The Devon Consol Mine was discovered in 1845 and was the richest copper mine in Europe for

The mud has built up a lot since the days when Weir Quay was a busy port

20 years and arsenic was also mined in the area. You could spend days exploring the quays along both banks of the Tamar for the relics of the industrial revolution that changed the whole aspect of the river but today the river has returned nearly to its pristine state with the main activity coming from yachting.

Access by road

To get to Weir Quay is something of a torturous journey out from Plymouth along mainly single track roads but is easier to reach from the A390 near Tavistock. Turn off south onto the B3257 and then turn left at Bere Alston where the road is signposted to Weir Quay. Postcode for the satnav is PL20 7BS.

Parking

Spaces along the road.

Water access

It is a straightforward run up the Tamar to Weir Quay and the boatyard offers a few moorings for visitors. One of the best ways to see Weir Quay is to take a trip up the River Tamar by water on one of the river steamers that run trips in the summer from Plymouth. The quays at Weir Quay are private as is most of the waterfront along this stretch of river.

Facilities

Apart from the boatyard chandlery there is little in the way of facilities at Weir Quay.

More information

There is a sailing club at www.weirquaysailingclub.co.uk and this occupies the site of the quay that served the limekiln. They cater mainly for dinghy sailing but also have moorings. The boatyard is at www.weir-quay.com ☎ 01822 840948

Comments

For its remoteness and peace and quiet Weir Quay is worth a visit. You can see the river from the road apart from where private houses occupy the land between the road and the river. One of the original quays that juts out into the deep water has warning notices saying that it is private and you get the feeling that Weir Quay wants to forget its past and settle into becoming a dormitory village for the nearby towns and a retirement centre. Today it is hard to picture the activity that must have taken place on the quay in its heyday as a port.

Now largely derelict, the Quay is private with only yachts for company

Gunnislake, River Tamar

Gunnislake was a significant village from early times because it was on the first bridge crossing of the River Tamar on what was then the main route into Cornwall. However, it was the discovery of copper in the hills above Gunnislake that really put it on the map. Great Consoles was the largest copper mine in the world and there were over 100 shafts sunk to exploit the mineral in this region. Although much of the ore was shipped out through Morwellham further down the Tamar, Gunnislake was the nearest port to many of the mines and so offered the shortest transport route even though access was not so easy.

Gunnislake lies at the head of navigation on the Tamar and there are three weirs across the river here. To bypass the weirs and to create the port at Gunnislake a short canal was built with a single lock at the entrance. This is now virtually all that remains of the port and the lock has been blocked off with the wooden gates hanging off their hinges. The lock keeper's cottage located on what is virtually an island between the canal and the river is still in use as a private house. The course of the canal can be followed through the woods but little remains of the loading wharves. It is likely that cargoes were carried down river by barges rather than by the trading ships judging by the size of the canal lock.

Access by road

From the main A390 road that runs through the village take the turning on the left going uphill on the west side of the river opposite the Cornish Inn. This is Calstock Road then turn left down Kingswood Road and then right onto Bealswood Road which becomes a lane and runs down to the canal. Postcode of the Cornish Inn is PL18 9BW to give a satnav guide.

Parking

There is some street parking in village but down Bealswood Road is a small area of free parking on the left which is the closest car access to the lock.

Water access

The remains of a winch used to open the lock gates at Gunnislake

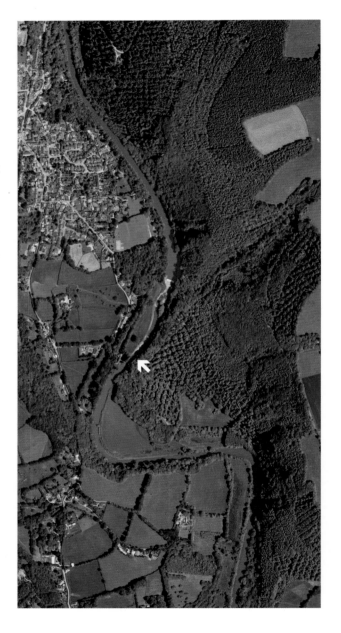

The lock is almost hidden amongst the trees

The Tamar runs on a winding course to just below Gunnislake where the first of the three weirs blocks the river. It is possible for a yacht to get up the winding river to the entrance to the canal but there is nothing in the way of moorings or landing access here. The river valley is very attractive and is an Area of Outstanding Natural Beauty.

Facilities
Gunnislake has shops and several pubs and most of the facilities of a large village. There is a scenic railway line running to Gunnislake from Plymouth.

More information
www.gunnislake.org

Comments
Gunnislake is another hidden harbour that has turned its back on its industrial past and turned to the tourist industry for a living. On the main road down to the river bridge from the east you can still see the mining chimneys on the northern skyline but trying to find the old canal and the associated wharves is a struggle. The old lock gives a fascinating glimpse into the past but with the historical focus now on the restored quays of Morwellham and Cothele further down river, the history of Gunnislake looks fated to fade away.

The old lock-keeper's house alongside the remains of the lock

Treluggan, River Lynher

The River Lynher runs inland from where the St Germans River splits with one arm heading west up to St Germans and the other heading north up to Lynher. The river was used over the centuries for the transport of a variety of cargoes mainly destined for the surrounding countryside and the rivers provided an easy route for passenger services to Plymouth. There are several wharves along the banks and many of these were developed to serve quarries that produced a hard rock used for construction projects such as the naval base at Plymouth. In the early 1900s a major quarry was developed at Treluggan about halfway up the river and a wharf was built to ship the stone out firstly by barge to Plymouth where it was transhipped onto coastal ships for transport around the UK and Europe.

The quarried stone was dug out and sent through chutes down to the wharves along the river and then

The railway viaduct spans the River Lynher just below the harbour

directly into the barges. The quarry became uneconomic in the 1970s because of its poor road connections and was closed down and the potential for establishing a marina on the site was explored. Today Treluggan is a full facility boatyard offering dry storage for yachts, whilst the marina section along the river attracts a wide variety of rather strange live-aboard vessels. The remains of the old wharves are still visible and provide the access track to the pontoons and boats moored alongside.

Access by road

Brown signs on the A38 at Landrake, some 10 miles west of Plymouth point to Boating World. Turn off just before the crest of the hill and follow these brown signs first to Trewint then to St Erney and then down a long winding single track road to Boating World, the name of the boat yard. Postcode for Boating World is PL12 5ES.

Parking

There is a small car park just before the entrance to the boatyard on the right hand side.

Water access

The best access is from half flood onwards and follow the river channel under the railway viaduct. The channel is marked but the reliability of the marks is not known. It may be possible to find a temporary berth alongside the pontoons but contact the boat yard first (☏ 01752 851515).

Facilities

There are full facilities at the yard for hauling out, storage and servicing. There is a café with a limited menu on site.

More information

www.boatingworldsw.co.uk

Comments

Despite lying in an Area of Outstanding Natural Beauty the boatyard looks a mess both on the extensive hard standing that was the location of the

Building long distance rowing boats at the specialist factory

The quay at Treluggan is home to many aging houseboats

old quarry and along the waters edge. The owners claim that they are starting to tidy the place up but the impression is that it still has a long way to go. This could be such an attractive spot and there is considerable potential. Several of the sheds are sub-let and one builds the ocean rowing boats that are used for such projects as rowing the Atlantic. There are plans for a conference centre and accommodation but there are no signs of much development. The boatyard claims to be the largest in the southwest.

St Germans

St Germans Quay framed by the railway viaduct

The Quay Sailing Club has their own gated section of the quay

St Germans started life as a fishing port which seems strange for a port so far inland. It developed as a cargo port in the 18th century when it was used to import coal, limestone and timber and export tin, copper and lead from the mines. The quay at St Germans was the main quay along the St Germans River because of the deeper water access but there were numerous quays along the river right up to Tideford which was the head of navigation before it silted up. It is likely that the quay at St Germans was used for bringing in cargoes by ship because of its deep water and these would then be transhipped into sailing barges for movement to the smaller quays that extended to the network of rivers in the region.

When most of the trade was switched to the railways, St Germans Quay was still used to ship out road stone from local quarries but today it has a boatyard, a sailing club and a wood yard. The magnificent railway viaduct that spans the river just upstream is a reminder of how the railways took over much of the trade of the port but in its heyday St Germans even boasted a ferry service that ran to Plymouth on market days. A reminder of the past can be seen in the limekilns that are still located along the back of the quay.

Access by road

From the Trerulefoot roundabout on the A38 take the A374 and then the B3249 to St Germans. The quay can be found down Quay Lane which turns off to the left after crossing the railway. Old Quay Lane is a turning before and leads down to the river where there was another small quay. Postcode for satnav PL12 5NA.

Parking

Limited parking on the road above the quay.

Water access

The St Germans River dries out at low water above Warren Point but the channel is marked by pole beacons and easy to follow as the tide rises and the railway viaduct gives a good guide.

Facilities

The quay is about a mile from the village itself where there are all the usual facilities including the Elliot Arms pub. The Quay sailing club welcomes visitors and overnight berths are available.

More information

www.quaysailingclub.co.uk

Comments

Compared with its active past the quay at St Germans is very quiet today with very little activity at the boatyard and the other businesses that are located there. You sense that the quay is ripe for development and if this happens it may loose any sense of history that remains today. The active sailing club perhaps points the way to where the future lies with leisure activities taking over from commercial use and the same has happened to many of the quays and villages along this network of picturesque and unspoilt rivers that meander into the hills to the west of Plymouth.

*The old buildings on the quay now form
part of a small industrial estate*

Portwrinkle, Whitsand Bay

Of all the harbours in this book Portwrinkle near Plymouth has to be one of the most amazing. It is on an open exposed beach and amazing because of its tiny size. It is barely big enough to moor a half a dozen boats and it looks more like a model harbour than a real one. As far as can be determined the harbour at Portwrinkle was built in the 17th century to provide some protection for the village fishing fleet that was engaged in the pilchard fishery.

It consists of two stone walls built out from the low cliff with the entrance protected by a loose rock breakwater that covers at high tide. Although it appears wide open to the southwesterly storms at high water, it is quite well protected by the off-lying rocks that help to break up the power of the waves before they reach the harbour. They certainly knew what they were doing when they built this harbour

One of the few fishermen who still operate out of Portwrinkle

The stone beacon off Portwrinkle does not mark anything specific

and unlike many other exposed ports Portwrinkle has stood the test of time.

Above the harbour the remains of the old fish cellars that were an essential part of the pilchard fishery are built into the walls of new buildings. Although Portwrinkle was mainly used for fishing it is likely that cargoes of coal and lime found there way here in later years.

Access by road

Take the A374 off the main A38 towards Torpoint and turn off right to Crafthole and Portwrinkle. Postcode for the Whitsand Bay Hotel is PL11 3BU.

Parking

Pay and display parking along the road above the cliffs in the village. There is also a private pay car park when you first enter the village that offers day long parking.

Water access

It would be possible to enter Portwrinkle by tender but it would be best to see the layout from the land first. There are ridges of off-lying rocks and a stone beacon built on the rocks but this lies well to the east of the entrance. The entry line would be roughly in line with the end of the houses in the village bearing 055°T and you are looking for the triangle beacon that marks the end of the outer breakwater. Do not cut this close as rocks extend out another 15 metres or so from the beacon. Then the very narrow entrance should be visible.

Facilities

The Whitsand Bay Hotel offers food, drink and accommodation and there is a kiosk in the private car park and the waterfront.

More information

www.cornwallbeachguide.co.uk/ caradon/portwrinkle

The almost circular harbour with the small outer breakwater guarding its narrow entrance

Comments

The harbour at Portwrinkle is a fascinating place and today there are only two or three small fishing boats operating from the port. They fish for crab and lobsters amongst the rocks rather than the pilchards for which the port was built and which are long gone. The rocky beach to the east of the harbour is called Finnygook Beach and whilst not much good for swimming it is a favourite with families because of its many rock pools. School parties also visit. Further east the long Whitsand Bay beach is a favourite with surfers.

Lostwithiel, River Fowey

It is hard to realise that the small town of Lostwithiel was once the main port of Cornwall and one of the major ports of Britain. Today the port, if we can still call it that, lies at the end of a shallow and narrow winding river that can only be negotiated by shallow draft and small vessels. In its past it was the only port to ship out Cornish tin and there are still the substantial remains of the 13th century buildings that were the focus of the trade. Like so many Cornish ports that were involved in shipping out the mineral wealth of the county it was the detritus of the mining that caused the harbour to silt up and by the 14th century Lostwithiel had lost much of its trade to the expanding port of Fowey at the river mouth.

The fine bridge across the river that marks the head of navigation dates back to 15th century and the quay where much of the trade took place still exists with many of the old buildings including the Stannary building still in place. The railway came to Lostwithiel in the 1800's and the town was one of the main railway workshops, a location on the river that has now been converted in to housing. The port was still in use up to the beginning of the Second World War with barges coming up the river from Fowey with coal and other materials but now is only a haven for a few small leisure craft.

The ancient bridge across the river that was the head of navigation

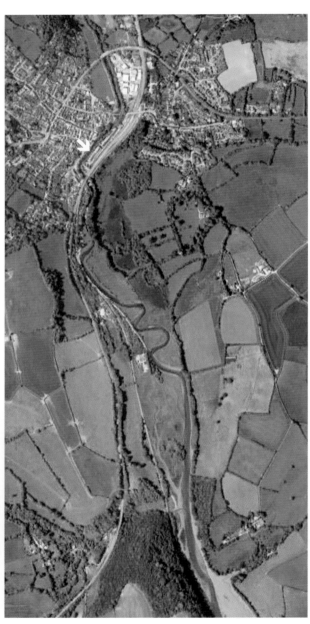

Access by road

Lostwithiel lies on the main A390 road between Liskeard and St Austell. Turn off to the left when heading west to find the harbour. Postcode for the satnav PL22 0HE.

Parking

Various parking spaces available around the town and on the quay itself.

Water access

The trip up the river Fowey is well worthwhile but the charts are poor as you head towards the town and a detailed Ordnance Survey map gives a better guide to the channel. The trip is best done on the flood tide near high water when it is possible to carry around 5 feet of water but this is really a dinghy trip. There are moorings along a concrete quay below the railway line as you approach the town.

Facilities

There are good restaurants and several pubs and hotels in the town and all the normal shopping facilities.

More information

www.lostwithieltic.org.uk

Comments

Lostwithiel is a fascinating town with a fascinating history. Today it has largely turned its back on the river and port and focuses on the main road through the town. A stroll down to the quay, under the railway bridge and on through a small park to the main mooring area helps to give a feel for the history of the port and what it was like, but there are no signs of the forest of sailing ship masts that once crowded the quays, and the water depths in the channel are more those of a shallow river than a bustling port.

An anchor from one of the last of the sailing barges that worked the river up until the Second World War

The remains of the river quay seen under the railway bridge

Pont, River Fowey

Pont is named after its bridge, the first crossing of Pont Creek that forks off to the east from Fowey Harbour. The footbridge marks the head of navigation of this inlet and it was here that a small wharf was established to discharge cargoes for the hamlet of Pont and for the adjacent farms. The wharves were built in the 18th and 19th centuries and have been well preserved and restored by the National Trust. Barges and small coasting ships would head up the shallow creek on the tide and lie aground at the quays for the cargoes to be discharged.

These cargoes were mainly inbound, comprising coal, lime, barley and fertiliser and there are the remains of two limekilns on the quay, one of them built into the hillside so that it could be loaded from

NOTICE

Dues for discharging or shipping over these quays will be collected as follows

Grain 1ᵈ per Quarter:
Timber 3ᵈ per Load.
Manures 3ᵈ per Ton.
Sand 2ᵈ Coal 3ᵈ

Other goods in like pro portion.

Wᴹ PEASE.
Steward.

Dated Lostwithiel, May 19th. 1894.

Charges for landing goods at Pont quay over a century ago

the top. There are old quarries further up the valley and stone could have been exported from these. The building on the main quay called The Farmhouse used to be a pub called The Ship but it is now two holiday cottages. There is a board on this building giving the landing charges for various cargoes and there is a pair of granite mooring posts still existing on the quay. Downstream from the built-up quay walls are the remains of an older quay that was created by levelling off the natural rock at the creek edge.

Evidence that Pont Creek was a busy place in the past comes from the old water mill a couple of hundred yards up the river from the bridge. To power the wheel, water was diverted from up-river and carried in a channel to the wheel and this can be seen from the road that leads to Pont. Today the hamlet of Pont is given over almost entirely to holiday homes but the charm of this hidden harbour remains to be discovered. Pont is in Du Maurier country and one of the wrecks in Pont Creek is thought to be that of the *Jane Slade* that featured in one of Daphne DuMaurier's first books.

Access by water

Pont is best visited by dinghy during the last three hours of a flood tide. The channel largely follows the outside of the bends in the creek and the change from the busy Fowey harbour to the tranquillity of Pont Creek is dramatic. You will see herons and egrets along the steep shoreline on the 15-minute trip up the creek. It is possible to tie up temporarily at the quay at or close to high water but there are no longer-term moorings.

Access by road

From the main road that runs to Bodinnick Ferry, turn off to the left at the red telephone box, sign-posted to Polruan. The single-track road twists downhill and at the bottom of the hill, turn right. After 500 yards a lane leads off to the right just before the road bridge over the river and Pont is 200 yards down here on the left.

Pont is also on the famous Hall Walk, that runs from Bodinnick to Polruan and this is the best way to get to Pont because parking nearby to Pont is difficult.

Parking

You may find a parking space just at the entrance to the side road that leads down to Pont but there is no designated parking area. Do not park in the passing places along the single-track road.

Facilities

There are no facilities at Pont and the nearest pubs, shop and cafés are in Polruan about a mile away near the entrance to Pont Creek.

Comments

Pont is a wonderful example of what small harbours were like in the past with its stone quay, the warehouses and limekiln close by. There were probably hundreds of small harbours like this that took cargoes as close as possible to the place where they were going to be used to reduce land transport. Pont has survived because it is in the hands of the National Trust and is now a peaceful backwater.

The restored quay at Pont – with the buildings now used as holiday lets

Pentewan, Mevagissey Bay

The development of Pentewan began because of the shipping congestion at the nearby port of Charleston. Work started in 1818 on the development of the dock but before that it had been a small fishing and cargo harbour sited at the mouth of the St Austell River where there were fish cellars and quarried stone was being shipped out. The construction of the new harbour involved increasing the size of the basin, building a pier to channel the water in the entrance and excavating a reservoir to hold water used to flush out the entrance channel. Silting of the entrance was a major problem even before the new harbour was built and continued to be a problem so much so that now the port is abandoned and there is no access to the sea.

Like so many harbours used for the export of mining products it was the silt from the mine washings coming down the river that caused much

A section of the Pentewan dock as it is today with no access to the sea

of the silting. In its heyday ships were calling with cargoes of coal and exports included tin and china clay. The port prospered when a railway was built down the valley from St Austell but this railway was

The remains of the lock gates that bridged the entrance channel

Comments

So much remains of the old harbour at Pentewan but it is now in a derelict state. The lock gates are still in place at the dock entrance and the winding gear for opening and shutting the gates can be seen amongst the weeds. Many of the rail tracks that served the harbour are still in place around the south side of the dock and the outer pier is still there. The village is centred around the dock, which looks like an overgrown village pond and it looks like the whole area went to sleep for 100 years and woke up in the modern world but without any access to the sea.

The remains of the breakwater wall with the silted channel behind it

never extended inland to the china clay pits that it was meant to serve. The opening of the harbour at Par sounded the death knell of Pentewan and the last china clay cargo was shipped out in 1929 and the last trading ship entered the harbour in 1940.

Access by road

Take the B3273 from the St Austell bypass signposted to Mevagissey and the turning for Pentewan is on the left after about 5 miles. Postcode for satnav PL26 6BX.

Parking

Limited free parking on the village side of the harbour.

Water access

The sand has completely closed the harbour entrance so the only water access is to land on the beach by dinghy. It is possible to anchor off except when the wind is between east and south.

Facilities

The Ship Inn alongside the dock serves food and drink. There is a café, a post office/store and a chandlery in the village. The beach to the south hosts a large caravan park and is well used as a holiday beach. Pentewan Sailing Club (www.pentewansailingclub.org.uk) hosts sailing races and dinghies and sports boats can be launched off the beach.

Devoran, River Fal

To look at Devoran today is to see a placid backwater that the world has passed by with hardly a boat in sight on the open stretches of estuary. Yet around 100 years ago Devoran was one of the busiest ports in the West Country. Located on the west side of the Fal estuary it was the closest port to the rich copper mines at Gwennap and it was developed when the Redruth and Chasewater Railway opened to create the rail link between the mines and the port. The village of Devoran was built up around the wharves, rather than the wharves developing as part of the village. The railway in the docks was operated by horses pulling the trucks along the spider's web of railway lines that served the many wharves along the waterfront.

The port itself started to be developed in 1838 and expanded rapidly with the ore being shipped out and a variety of cargoes such as coal, lime, timber

The restored remains of the old hoppers where the ore from the mines was dumped from rail trucks

and building materials coming in. The ore was tipped from the railway trucks into hoppers that can still be seen today and from there it was transferred to the ships. As a major port Devoran only survived for around 40 years and then fell into decline as the output from the mines petered out and the estuary silted up. Nearby Perranarworth was the destination for many of the Norwegian timber ships that brought in pit props for the mines and the local pub there is still called the Norway Inn.

Access by road

A turning off the main A39 at the round-about is signposted to Devoran and leads directly into the village. The lower Old Quay Road through the village eventually leads to a park that in turn gives access to the waterfront. Postcode for the satnav is TR3 6ND.

Parking

Very limited along the road by the park or in the village.

Water access

Harbour has silted badly and the fact that there are virtually no boats moored in the river or at the old quays suggests that the harbour is little used. The channel winds up the creek and is not marked so this is now a harbour to visit by dinghy rather than by yacht and then only around high-water.

Facilities

There is a reminder of the past in the Old Quay pub above the jetties and the village has a shop and post office.

More information

www.devoran.co.uk

Comments

Devoran today seems to be trying to cover up its past. There is little attempt to promote or highlight its industrial history and the village turns its back on

The restored quay now with a wooden facing

the waterfront except for dog walkers who use the grassed over wharf area. The remains of the wharves can be clearly seen but they have been made safe using a wooden facing rather than the original stone but some of the original granite mooring posts still remain. The road is still called Old Quay Road and further along is the Old Tram Road that heads towards some old wharves further east. A few yachts moor in a loading basin along the wharves but there is little sense of the once very busy port and the bustling river than existed in its heyday.

An old granite bollard left after the quay has disintegrated

Port Navas, Helford River

The old limekiln

The upper reaches are now a quiet backwater with the quay walls still visible

The small creek and village of Port Navas on the north side of the Helford River is now an oasis of calm with an industrial past. The creek itself was probably used by small coastal ships to bring in coal and limestone and a limekiln on the quay by the yacht club suggests this was the site of the first quay in the creek. The main development in the port was the building of Port Navas Quay in the 18th century as a base to ship out the much sought after Constantine Granite. This very hard granite was reputed to have been used in the construction of Nelson's Monument and Tower Bridge in London. By the early 20th century the granite trade had died but more recently the quay has been used as a landing place for some of the Helford oyster fisheries with a processing plant attached.

The village has now been 'gentrified' and the track down to the quay is not sign-posted but lies on the east side of the creek past the Port Navas Yacht Club. The quay that now serves the oyster fishery and the limekiln are now the only remains of what must have been a thriving little harbour.

Access by road

Long winding single track roads signposted from Constantine in the west and Mawnan Smith in the east. Postcode for satnav TR11 5RJ.

Parking

Very limited street parking on the approach road on the west side of the village.

Water access

From the main Helford River, Port Navas lies off to the right up a channel that virtually dries at low water. The channel is marked by buoys and these lead into Port Navas creek and to the yacht club pontoons. Anchoring or grounding in the approach channels could interfere with the oyster beds and lead to fines for damage.

Facilities

Nothing in the village and the yacht club has the only bar and other facilities.

More information

Port Navas Yacht Club ☎ 01326 340065
www.portnvasyachtclub.co.uk
Helford river moorings
www.helfordrivermoorings.co.uk

*The disputed oyster processing
facility at the old river quay*

Comments

The lack of facilities at Port Navas suggest that visitors are not encouraged but the yacht club is the centre of social activity with some visitors berths available and visits by tenders are encouraged. The creek is quite beautiful and quiet with small yachts lining the east side and well worth a visit, but there is local controversy over the oyster quay which is said to resemble an industrial unit that is out of character with the quiet peace of the river. It can be equally argued that the oyster trade is what developed the Helford River's prosperity and here is a prime example of the clash between traditional and new that has become a feature of the Helford River.

Trelowarren, Helford River

The quay at Trelowarren is almost hidden amongst the trees

The Trelowarren Estate is based around a stately home that dates back several centuries and has been in the same family for five centuries. It lies up the valley at the head from one arm of Mawgan Creek and just by the old stone bridge over the creek lies a disused stone quay. This is one of the very few quays remaining virtually original that were a feature of nearly every creek and river in Cornwall. A stone building on the quay would have been the store for cargoes brought in or ready for shipment and quays like this were the destination of small coastal sailing ships that would have brought in coal, perhaps building materials and manure or limestone for the farms and taken out timber or agricultural produce.

There are the remains of three such quays on Mawgan Creek, Bishops Quay near the mouth of the creek and the farm quay at the head of the other arm of the creek. The creek virtually dries out at low water and is hemmed in by trees coming right down to the water's edge. Today the creek is almost empty of boats with just a few boats associated with houses along the creek. There are the remains of ancient settlements in the area and these creeks provided access for small trading ships to many of the rural areas.

Access by road

Follow the unclassified road east from the village of Mawgan which in turn lies east of the B3293.

Parking

Very limited parking just to the west of the bridge over the creek.

Water access

Because of trees that have fallen in the water and not been cleared plus the shoaling of the creek the trip upstream from the Helford River is best done by dinghy on the flood tide, but it is well worth the trip for the peace and quiet that you find at the quay.

Facilities

No facilities, but Trelowarren House, which is a short walk up the valley, has a café and there is a pub and restaurant in Mawgan village half a mile away.

Comments

Trelowarren is a hidden gem that the world seems to have passed by. Its current state of neglect has helped to retain its character and charm and combined with the ancient bridge it is well worth a visit just to get a feel for the past and what it must have been like along the Helford River 200 years ago. It is easy to picture small ships alongside the quay tied up to the granite bollards and loading or discharging cargoes for the local communities.

The quay is now almost derelict but the small warehouse is used for storage

The quiet creek leading up to Trelowarren at low water

Gillan Harbour, Helford River

Gillan Harbour is in fact several villages around this creek to the south of the Helford River including Flushing, St Anthony, Gillan Cove and Carne up at the head of the creek. These villages all had small quays where trading ships would have discharged mainly coal and limestone and load fish and agricultural produce. There is evidence that the Romans established a base here and to look at modern day Gillan Creek it is hard to believe that much has changed. Gillan is well off the beaten track and is all the more beautiful because if it. The commercial shipping and the fishing fleets of the past have had very little lasting impact on this secluded backwater except for some modern housing development around Gillan itself.

The church at St Anthony

An old quay on the south side of the harbour

Access by road

It is all single track roads around here with high hedges and you need to have faith in your satnav to find the hamlets around the creek. TR12 6JW takes you to St Anthony and from there you can follow round the creek but water access is very limited.

Parking

Very difficult in most places but there is a pay and display car park in St Anthony which is the best water access for the area.

Water access

A straightforward entrance apart from Car Croc rock, which is marked by a buoy. There are many mooring buoys in the main section of the harbour and even before you reach St Anthony this is a harbour that mainly dries out at low water but the sheer beauty of the creek makes it well worth exploring by dinghy.

Facilities

None apart from Sailaway, a boat and yacht hire business in St Anthony who also should be contacted regarding moorings in the creek. Small boats can be rented from Sailaway for those wanting to explore the creek by water.

More information

Sailaway ☎ 01326 231 357
info@stanthony.co.uk

The foreshore at St Anthony with the old warehouse and pontoon now used by Sailaway

Comments

One of the best 'get away from it all' harbours on the Cornish coast but it is so far removed from the mainstream that it can be hard to get access. Its remoteness is its attraction and St Anthony is probably the best place to stop and follow the footpaths to get a picture of this beautiful creek. Here you can climb the hill above the compact village and look down on the creek.

Porthoustock, Falmouth Bay

Porthoustock is unusual in that it was developed later than most small harbours and is still in commercial use today. Before its commercialisation it was a small fishing community locked in the sheltered cove but when demand for granite developed in the mid to late 1800s for building ports and harbours the stone at the adjacent quarries was exploited. The quarries were on both sides of the cove with the first loading tip on the north side. The tramways connected both quarries to the loading tip and the remains of the track can still be seen on the north side above the cove. The north quarry was abandoned and all quarrying moved to the southern quarry and a new jetty was built so ships could load alongside. This jetty is still in use today and as well as small stone the quarry can also supply large rocks for reinforcing harbour walls and jetties and this can be delivered directly to site by tug and barges.

The fishing is still active, mainly after crabs and lobsters and the fishermen haul their boats up the shingle beach with small powered winches in wooden sheds under the cliff. A lifeboat was established here in the late 1800s to go to the aid of ships stranded on the notorious Manacles Rocks a mile offshore, but this area is now served by the Falmouth and Lizard lifeboats.

Access by road

Join the B3293 from Helston to St Keverne and after St Keverne follow the single track road to Porthoustock. Postcode for the satnav is TR12 6QW.

Parking

On the top of the beach – request for payment but no enforcement.

Water access

The old quarry tip on the north side of the cove is a good guide in. The only off-lying danger is the Manacle Rocks. The cove is sheltered except from winds from the east sector and beach landing is possible by dinghy.

A ship loader at the new quay waiting for the next ship

The beach is now dominated by the old concrete ship loader with the new quay across the bay

Facilities

None but facilities available in St Keverne a mile and a half inland.

Comments

Porthoustock is a fascinating place partly because it is still a commercial port and partly because the tourist industry has not caught up with it. The local fishermen seem to operate comfortably alongside the quarry operations, although there is a certain amount of noise and dust from the quarry but this is largely hidden from the village itself at the head of the cove. Visits by ships are quite rare with the quarry owners suggesting that this happens about every 6 months.

A section of the old railway line that was used to bring rock from the quarries to the loading quay

Lamorna, Mounts Bay

Lamorna Cove was a small fishing hamlet on the exposed Cornish coastline west of Penzance until the granite on the nearby headland was found to be some of the hardest in the county. That led to the opening up of the quarry on the hill above the cove both on the east and the west side of the cove and the use of the small harbour for ships that came to load the granite. The small curving breakwater was built to create the harbour but it did not offer a great deal of shelter for the sailing ships loading in the harbour so that they would have to keep a very close eye on the weather. The cove is a lee shore in the prevailing southwesterlies that could be the herald of bad weather and swell rolling in from the Atlantic must have been a major problem.

For the fishermen that used the cove for generations the breakwater offered enough protection for them to launch and recover their boats on the beach inside the harbour and to haul them up above the tide line. There are still some boats using the harbour in this way but they are for leisure rather than commercial use. The quarry was opened up in 1861 and the stone blocks would be brought down to the breakwater quay for loading by horse and cart. The best known use of the Lamorna granite is for the construction of the Thames Embankment. The remote location of Lamorna made it an ideal place for smuggling and this is reflected in the name of the local pub, the Lamorna Wink, where a wink would produce a glass of smuggled brandy.

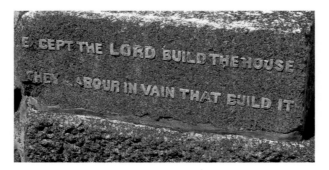

A quotation let into the granite of the harbour wall

Today the beauty of Lamorna Cove is given over almost entirely to holiday makers and their requirements. Lamorna was also the home of several artists of the Newlyn School, which brought it fame outside Cornwall.

Access by road

Take the B3315 out of Penzance heading SW, past Mousehole and the sign for Lamorna will be seen on the left. After that it is a single track road down to the cove. The postcode for satnav navigation is TR19 6XH.

Parking

There is payment parking right by the harbour but another option if you are using the pub is to park there and walk down.

Water access

The approaches to Lamorna are straight forward. The small white lighthouse on Tater-du a mile to the west gives a guide and it is possible to anchor in the cove in settled weather and land by tender. There is no protection when the wind is from any direction south of east and west.

Facilities

The pub up the road offers food and drink and there is a restaurant at what was the Lamorna Hotel. On the quay there is a café and kiosk.

Comments

Lamorna Cove is stunningly beautiful, a real gem and a harbour that has changed very little over the past century except that it now caters for the holiday maker rather than commercial interests. The beach is pebbles and rocks except at low water when sand appears. One has to wonder how much longer the breakwater will survive because on a recent visit a large section of the outer rocks on the exposed wall had been washed away giving waves a toehold to create further destruction. The structure is a Grade II listed building but the owner claims he has no money for repairs and with no commercial interests there may not be enough financial incentive for repairs.

The remains of the old quarries dominate the skyline above Lamorna Cove

The shortened stone breakwater protects what is now the holiday beach at Lamorna

Priest's Cove, Cape Cornwall

The slipway with the Brisons rocks in the distance

Cove boats now use the slipway at Priest's Cove

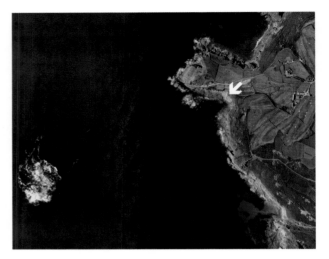

The Priest's Cove or Priest's Hole landing at Cape Cornwall has been a hidden harbour for local fishermen as far as records go back. It is one of the few places where it is possible to launch and recover a small boat along the rugged coastline between Sennen Cove and St Ives and the cove gains some protection from the Brisons rocks offshore. When the minerals started to be exploited along this section of the Cornish coast the mine operators must have looked closely at the possibility of bringing the trading ships into the cove with supplies of coal and to export the minerals. However, the cove is very vulnerable to the swell that comes in from the Atlantic and as the ships would have had to take the bottom when loading and discharging there might be only be a few days in the year when this was possible with safety. Fishermen with their small cove boats that would be hauled clear of the water would have no such problems and their launch and recovery has been made easier with the recent construction of a concrete slipway.

Old sloping tracks can be seen above the cove and these may have been the tracks of tramways from the mines above down to the cove. The tower on the top of the Cape is in fact a chimney from one of the mine engines. On the north side of Cape Cornwall there is some evidence to show that ships came into clefts in the rocks there so there is every likelihood that the same thing happened at Priest's Cove when the weather conditions allowed.

Access by road

From the village of St Just on the B3306 coast road take the sign posted Cape Cornwall Road just by the clock tower. Follow this road round several sharp bends down the hill and turn off into the car park at the bottom.

Parking

The is a National Trust car park at the end of the road and this pay car park is the only parking available.

Water access

You could land here by tender but trying to find a safe anchorage offshore could be difficult except in very settled conditions. There is a passage inside the Brisons from the south and access from the north is close round Cape Cornwall. In any offshore winds the area would be dangerous with the swell indicating the danger as it breaks on the rocks. Coming into the landing there can be a breaking swell that is clear to see from the land but not so obvious from seaward. The chimney on the hill above Cape Cornwall is a good guide to identify the place.

Facilities

There is a kiosk in the car park that serves snacks and drinks and further up the hill the Cape Cornwall Golf Club is open to visitors with excellent food and a bar. The village of St Just has pubs, hotels and restaurants but it is a mile up the hill.

More information

St Just Tourist Office ✆ 01736 788669.

Comments

Priest's Hole takes you by surprise and you are only aware that there are boats and a slipway when you are almost on top of them. This is a quite magical place and whilst there are perhaps a dozen cove boats parked at the top of the slipway only a couple of them are used for commercial fishing these days. The winch house at the top of the slipway has been restored but around this is a random group of stone huts that have been used as fishermen's' stores in the past. Any evidence that sailing cargo ships might have used the landing in the past has gone but you can't help feeling that there would have been some ships captains who would have been willing to try. However the Atlantic swell coming in from the west would have posed a constant danger.

The buildings above the cove with the tower that was a chimney for the boiler house of a mine

Portreath, North Cornwall

Portreath is a great example of a harbour that was created out of virtually nothing in order to ship ore out and bring coal in to Cornwall. It wasn't even built close to the mines but it was on the north side of Cornwall, which made it that much closer to the coal supplies from South Wales. Safe ports are rare on the north coast of Cornwall and ports like Portreath saved the long and dangerous voyage around Land's End.

Construction of the port started in 1760 when a pier was built out alongside the small river that ran through Portreath. This created a small harbour alongside the eastern cliff and in 1801 the first of the inner basins was constructed to give better shelter from onshore winds. This inner basin was connected by a tramway with cast iron rails that ran right across Cornwall, connecting the port to several of the major inland mines. The second inner basin was built later and was connected to an inclined railway that took coal up and copper ore down from the Portreath branch of the Hayle railway, giving Portreath the distinction of having two railway connections to make it a major trans-shipment port.

There were shipyards in the port and at its peak over 100,000 tons of ore were shipped from Portreath in one year. Commercial shipping still used the port up to 1960 but now it is occupied by mainly fishing and angling boats. For sailing ships, it must have been a nightmare entrance requiring total commitment to sail into the narrow entrance with the hope that dropping the anchor would stop the ship before it hit something.

The lookout hut above the harbour at Portreath

Access by road
Portreath lies on the coast road, the B3300 going in from the east and the B3301 from the west. The postcode for the satnav is TR16 4NQ.

Parking
Pay and display car park on the sea front.

Water access
The conspicuous white day mark on the cliff to the east of the entrance helps to identify Portreath from seaward and the 60 foot high Gull Rock lies to the west. Entrance is possible either side of high water with the entrance channel lying close to the pier but should only be attempted in settled weather. There are possible berths alongside in both basins but they dry out at low water.

The difficult entrance that must have been a considerable challenge for ships trying to enter

Facilities

Bassett Arms and Waterfront Inn pubs. Numerous kiosks, cafés and small shops. Post office/stores.

More information

Portreath Harbour Association
☎ 01209 890318.

Comments

Portreath has an amazing history as a port and whilst much of the original remains, the modern surroundings of the harbour have largely destroyed the atmosphere of the place. The village is now comprised of modern characterless holiday homes and you need to turn your back on these to get a feel of what the port was like. The remains of the old tramway and the inclined railway can still be seen and the port is largely intact with its spending beach in the outer harbour to break the force of any incoming waves, its granite mooring posts and the raised lookout tower built to watch for incoming ships.

Today Portreath harbour is surrounded by mediocre housing that takes away the character of the harbour

Trevaunance Cove, St Agnes

Trevaunance Cove has one of the most amazing histories as a port, having been built five times and washed away a similar number of times. It was the determination to have a port close by the site of some of Cornwall's most important tin mines that lead to this constant rebuilding, but today all that remains is a big pile of dressed granite blocks on the sands under the cliff and the remains of the infrastructure for the loading and discharge of ships.

The bay here is one of the few places on this North Cornish coast to offer some protection from the prevailing southwesterly storms. That and its proximity to the mines that can still be seen on the cliffs above lead to the building of the first port in 1632. That one was destroyed even before it was finished and it was 50 years before another attempt was made. This time it was located nearer the headland and tucked in more and that one was

The dressed stones that are all that remains of the harbour built at Trevaunance Cove

completed but was then destroyed in a storm. For the next attempt just a few years later they called in the famous engineer Winstanley but even he could not tame the waves and his harbour only lasted 6 years. However, he gained from the experience and on his next attempt he tied the granite blocks with iron bars. That one lasted 20 years and was rebuilt again in 1793 and lasted over 100 years. It only succumbed to the storms when a damaged section was left unrepaired so that in 1915 the north pier collapsed again. By this time road and rail transport were taking over anyway and the requirement for a port was less important. Coal from South Wales was landed at the harbour and the tin ore taken out on the return.

At its peak in the 18th century, Trevauance Cove must have been a hive of activity with water wheels in the village stream driving a hammer mill for iron forging, the mines on the hills above and the loading and discharge of the ships with the ore being dropped down the cliff face into the ships.

Access by road

From the village of St Agnes take the sign-posted road to the beach that is on the left at the roundabout at the bottom of the hill in the one way system and the cove is half a mile down there. Postcode for the satnav TR5 0RT.

Parking

A pay and display car park is located on the left just 300 yards from the cove. There is a second smaller payment car park just above the beach.

Water access

A beach landing only with clear water after rounding St Agnes Head. The beach is very popular with surfers.

Facilities

The Driftwood Spars is a 17th-century pub with a micro brewery and accommodation. There are also cafés and kiosks. Full facilities in St Agnes. Surfboards and suits for hire. An RNLI inshore lifeboat station and lifeguards.

More information

www.stagnes.com

Comments

Trevaunance Cove has completely moved away from its industrial past today and is purely a pleasure beach with a few boats operating off the beach. It is a beautiful spot and the remains of the harbour are still on the west side of the beach, now mainly a pile of big stones and boulders and the remains of the north pier foundations can still be seen. On the cliffs above the remains of some of the loading and transport infrastructure to and from the mines can still be seen.

The beautiful beach with the harbour remains in the foreground

Only the remains of the old pier head have been left standing by the waves

Wadebridge, River Camel

An old stone bollard replanted away from the quay at Wadebridge

The sign on the bridge over the River Camel

In the past harbours were established as far inland as possible when water transport was the most economical means of moving bulk cargoes. They also tended to be close to where the first bridge crossing of a river was established and Wadebridge scores on both of these aspects. The town was originally known as Wade but when the bridge was built in 1468 it became Wadebridge. The original bridge was just 9 feet wide and is reputed to have been built on wool foundations. The 17 arch bridge was widened in 1853 and again in 1963 when the traffic congestion on the main A39 road became a traffic nightmare.

The main harbour was located on the west side of the River Camel close by the bridge and the line of the wharves can still be seen today although it has been fully rebuilt and sheet steel piled. All of the old wharf buildings have gone to be replaced by trendy housing and apartments. The river splits in the harbour area at Wadebridge and the eastern channel also serves a series of wharves that today resemble an industrial estate with little connection to the river. Cargo coming into Wadebridge would have been coal from South Wales and the return cargoes would have been mainly farm produce. Sand was also dredged from the river and landed at the quays for onward transport to farms to help lighten the soil.

The coming of the railway to Wadebridge in 1834 marked a turning point for the harbour and took away much of the cargo. Padstow, downriver was

also a more convenient port in many ways and the dreaded Doom Bar across the entrance to the River Camel was another deterrent to trade.

Access by road

Wadebridge lies on the main A39 road but today the town is by-passed so you need to turn off the main road for access to the town.

Parking

There are several pay and display car parks in the town. Alternatively there is some street parking on the east side of the bridge allowing a walk across the bridge into the town centre

Water access

First you have to negotiate the Doom Bar at the entrance and this is not advisable in onshore winds. The channel is well marked as far as Padstow but after that it is largely a question of following the yacht moorings. When construction work on the town quay is finished it may be possible to moor alongside there.

Facilities

Wadebridge has all the facilities of a small town with pubs and cafés on both sides of the river. There is a small boatyard at the north end of the town quay.

More information

www.destination-cornwall.co.uk/wadebridge
Padstow harbourmaster covers the area.
☏ 01841 532239

Comments

The River Camel is a fascinating river and the Camel Trail that follows the line of the old railway route along the west bank is a popular tourist attraction and gives a good feel for what the river was like in the past. Wadebridge is also a fascinating town but much of its marine history has been destroyed but you can find a recovered granite bollard re-established in a small park at the eastern end of the bridge. Hopefully facilities for yachts will be provided once the Town Quay rebuilding is finished but at present this looks very private and inaccessible and the town seems to want to ignore its maritime history.

The old quay is now being rebuilt to support the apartment blocks that have replaced the old warehouses

Port Quin, North Cornwall

Looking to seaward from the quay at Port Quin

The rocky foreshore in the harbour with the harbour buildings now converted to holiday homes

Port Quin is one of the few harbours in the South West that has remained virtually unchanged over the centuries even though its use has changed considerably. Because of its remoteness it was never a commercial harbour for cargoes except perhaps very occasional cargoes of coal and lime for local use but it relied mainly on its pilchard fishing for survival. The income from fishing would no doubt be supplemented by smuggling where its remote location was a major benefit.

This tiny inlet is exposed to the north west with the offshore Cow and Calf Rocks offering minimal shelter. The village was nearly abandoned when the pilchard shoals did not arrive one year and then the fishing fleet was decimated one night in 19th century when a violent storm caught the fleet out at sea and from which it is reported that there were no survivors. Following this the village was abandoned with the women and children going nearby Port Issac. The hamlet has been revived under the ownership of the National Trust and is a fascinating place to visit. It seems to have hardly changed over the years although it is now probably much tidier that when it was a fishing port.

On the western headland Doyden Castle overlooks the entrance and this was built in the 18th century as a retreat by a local businessman and is reputed to have been the scene of wild parties and gambling. Today it is a National Trust holiday home like the cottages in the village.

Access by road

From the B3314 Wadebridge to Delabole road take the signposted roads to Port Quin.

Parking

At a pay National Trust car park behind the houses and slip.

Water access

Straightforward apart from the Cow and Calf Rocks that are visible at all states of tide. Anchorage in settled conditions is possible just inside the entrance.

There is a concrete launching slip for local boats but the beach is rocky and the landing could prove difficult in all except settled conditions.

Facilities

None.

More information

National Trust.

Comments

Port Quin has a very historic feel and little seems to have changed over the years except the concrete slipway and the use of the houses, which are now virtually all holiday homes. The old fish cellars remain and it is only some newer houses up the hill that make you realise that you have not stepped back 100 years in time. In the usual National Trust restoration style you get the feeling that the emotion and character of the place has been lost now it is no longer a working harbour but it is still well worth a visit.

The narrow entrance to Port Quin with the Cow and Calf rocks in the distance

Port Gaverne, North Cornwall

Port Gaverne is a wonderful example of a significant harbour created out of virtually nothing. Gaverne has been overshadowed by its near neighbour Port Issac where breakwaters were built to increase the shelter but Gaverne was the much more important port 150 years ago. The secret of its success was that it was closer to the slate quarries of Delabole and within more level transport distance so that the need for a port was more intense and Port Gaverne is probably one of the most creative ports in this book.

Situated on an inlet that is sheltered from the southwesterlies is was simply an open beach cove where fishing was the main industry and where sailing ships landed coal and limestone directly onto the beach. The old limekilns are still there at the head of the inlet and the old fish cellars remain but

The quay that was cut out of the solid cliff with the village in the distance

to create a wharf for loading the slate they simply carved away the cliff on the east side to form a wide ledge, smoothed off the vertical face and that was the jetty. It is still largely intact and the granite bollards still remain as does the inclined slope that was later cut into the cliffs to provide an access route for the horse and cart transport from the quarry.

Being wide open to the northwest the port had to be evacuated it when the wind went round in this direction and even in southwesterlies the heavy swell was a problem. However the port prospered until the railway came nearby. That caused the slate trade by sea to halt almost overnight in favour of the more reliable railway.

Access by road
On the B3314 turn off to the right on the signposted road after Delabole. The postcode for the Port Gaverne Hotel is PL29 3SQ.

Parking
There is a large pay and display car park on the headland between Port Gaverne and Port Issac.

Water access

After passing the large off-lying Gull Rock you can head straight in and it is possible to anchor off and land by tender on the beach when conditions are settled.

Facilities

There are kiosks on the beach road and the Port Gaverne Hotel provides meals, drink and accommodation.

More information

www.portissace-online.co.uk covers both Port Issac and Port Gaverne.

Comments

Port Gaverne still retains a quiet unspoilt appeal, certainly compared with its busy and congested neighbour and is well worth a visit. There is enough of the old port infrastructure remaining to give a feel of what it must have been like in its heyday although these days Port Gaverne has become just a quiet sophisticated holiday resort with just a few fishing boats operating from the beach.

Modern boats launch from the beach but ships would moor alongside the dressed stone quay

The track leading to the quay was cut out from the solid rock

Hartland Quay, Hartland Point

Hartland looks like an impossible place to build a harbour. Facing west and exposed to the storms from the open Atlantic and surrounded by daunting cliffs, Hartland Quay is an example of how desperate people were to bring bulk cargoes in by sea. It is thought that three of Britain's famous sailors, Sir Francis Drake, Sir Walter Raleigh and Sir John Hawkins financed the building of Hartland Quay in the 16th century as a port of refuge on this inhospitable coast, but it would have been so difficult to enter in a storm that its main purpose must have been to bring in cargoes to this stretch of coast.

It is an amazing tiny little harbour that was just about big enough to berth a couple of trading coasters. In a westerly wind it would have required total commitment to make the harbour entrance on this lee shore. Cargoes coming in were mainly coal and limestone from South Wales plus some building materials and the limekiln on the quay shows the main reason for the cargoes with the lime being used on the surrounding farms. The harbour was in constant need of repair because of the battering from Atlantic storms and when the railway provided an alternative overland route the harbour fell into disrepair and the sea won the battle. Today the slipway down to the harbour and the remains of the limekiln can still be seen but the harbour walls are now just a pile of boulders although the line of the breakwaters can still be seen.

The remains of the rocks used to build the harbour

Sign on the slipway at Hartland Quay

Access by road

From the A39 coast road take the B3248 to Hartland. Then follow the road to Stoke and then onwards to Hartland Quay. Postcode for the satnav is EX39 6DU.

Parking

It is a private road down to the Hartland Quay Hotel and you pay for parking at the top. There is plenty of parking at the hotel halfway down the sloping cliff.

Water access

It would be possible to anchor off and land by dinghy is settled weather. The old ramp down to the harbour is also used for launching local boats.

Facilities

The Hartland Quay Hotel offers food, drinks and accommodation. There is also a museum and a shop amongst the cluster of buildings at the head of the road down to the slipway.

More information

www.hartlandquayhotel.com

Comments

You can still get a feel for what it must have been like when the harbour was operational and you have to admire the tenacity of the people who landed cargoes and then had to get them up the cliff to the villages and farms nearby. The scenery along this coast is stunning and Hartland Quay is well worth a visit to admire both the past and the present. Having a drink in the Hotel gardens when the sun is setting in the west is one of life's pleasures.

The scattering of rocks is all that remains of the harbour with a cleared section to allow boats to launch

Buck's Mills, Barnstaple Bay

Winches used to recover boats from the beach below the eastern limekiln

Buck's Mills is the most amazing place and is another example of creating a harbour on a very inhospitable coastline. In the 15th century there were attempts to build a harbour at Buck's Mills and there was a degree of shelter available from a naturally occurring spit of rocks, the Gore, that runs out from the coast just to the west of Buck's Mills. The harbour was built to the east of this and large quantities of gunpowder were used to blast out the rocks. The harbour did not last long and succumbed to the ravages of the sea so that Buck's Mills then relied on the cargo boats beaching in a gut that was blasted out from the foreshore rocks.

This gut can be seen today at low water and both coal and limestone were landed on the beach. It must have been a skilful skipper who would undertake such a landing and be confident that he could get off again before the weather turned. This was a summer only exercise and the coal and limestone were burnt in two limekilns built under the cliffs that can still be seen today and the rough roads down to the beach still exist. Fishing boats also operated off the beach and still do today. Buck's Mills got its name from the water mill driven by the stream that ran down the valley that was used to grind corn.

Access by road

From the A39 coast road turn off at Buck's Cross and follow the long winding road down to the sea.

Parking

There is a free car park located on the right hand side of the road just above the village.

Water access

The best approach is directly from the north avoiding the long finger of the Gore stretching out to seaward for about half a mile to the west. Landing by dinghy only and then only with care because of extensive rocks either side of the gut.

Facilities

There are no facilities in Buck's Mills.

Comments

Buck's Mills is a fascinating place and another remarkable example of creating a harbour out of virtually nothing because of the need to import raw materials. After a somewhat chequered history it has now retired into a peaceful village and apart from the car park it does not try to attract visitors. However, it is very worthwhile to visit Buck's Mills if only to marvel at the ingenuity that created the harbour and the landing facilities that are still used by fishermen today.

The Gore still extends out to seaward to the west of Buck's Mills

The western limekiln and the steep access track to the stony beach

Braunton (Velator), Barnstaple Bay

Braunton claims to be the largest village in England and has a history extending back to the Stone Age and the Great Field adjacent to the creek is a classic example of a medieval British settlement. The creek on which Braunton stands extends inland from the River Taw and is the River Caen. In the past it was an important trading port, initially serving the local trade but later involved in international trade as well. Despite the challenging entrance to the Rivers Taw and Torridge over the west facing Appledore Bar, Braunton prospered as a port, shipping out farm produce and importing coal, lime and other materials.

It was the building of the quay at Velator in the 17th century just down river from the village that opened up the port to larger ships, enabling ships of up to 130 tons to use the port. These were the size of ships that could cross the Atlantic and there was regular trade across to Ireland although most of the trade from Braunton was across the Bristol Channel. Even in the 1930's the port was still in use, mainly with the importing of coal, sand and gravel and the export of scrap metal and the port was busy during the Second World War but after that the decline set in. Today the creek is a shadow of its former self with silting reducing the size of the channel and variety of yachts mooring along the banks and on moorings.

Braunton is reputed to be the last place where the sailing coasters of the Bristol Channel operated from and the village has a long history of ship-owning and operating. It is this local involvement that probably led to the way Braunton expanded as a port and why it lasted so long.

Access by road

Braunton lies on the main A361 road but to reach Velator you need to turn off left after crossing the river bridge. Cross the roundabout and another bridge and that road follows the creek.

Houseboats now occupy many of the inlets where coastal shipping used to land cargoes

The quay at Braunton and the narrow creek

Parking

There is a free parking area adjacent to the quay where the road widens.

Water access

Access is challenging with the Bideford Bar to negotiate before entering the marked channel. Do not pass too close to Crow Point because of off-lying rocks and then follow the River Taw channel. The creek entrance can be indentified as it lies just to the west of the RAF Chivenor airport.

Leisure boats now use the creek but there is no control over the moorings

Facilities

There are shops, pubs and hotels in the village but little in the way of facilities for visiting yachts.

More information

www.brauntontic.co.uk

Comments

It is quite sad to see the decline of the creek at Braunton and you get the feeling that the village has turned its back on its maritime heritage. There is no control over mooring in the creek so it tends to get used by boats in decline looking for free moorings. As boating expands there may be the possibility that the creek will find a new life but that will mean expanding shore facilities and imposing new buildings on what is an attractive remote location. Try to visit at high water when the creek looks a lot more attractive that the mud at low water. The airfield at Chivenor across the way is not as busy as in the past but it does create a background of aircraft noise.

Watermouth Harbour, Bristol Channel

The quay buildings with castle above

The harbourmaster's building on the quay

Watermouth Harbour is a natural inlet from the rugged North Devon coast and with the entrance facing north west it offers reasonable shelter in most conditions. Historically the harbour was used as a fishing port and for bringing in cargoes of coal and limestone but to all intents and purposes it is a drying harbour with virtually no quays except the wall across the top end of the harbour. The bottom of the harbour is mainly hard sand so trading ships would dry out and their cargoes landed into horse carts on the beach.

Entering Watermouth in any sort of a blow would require seamanship of the highest order. Once inside the entrance there is little room to turn and little room to stop and the sailing ships would drop an anchor to stop their progress and this would swing them round heading out to sea. From there the ships would be towed in by rowing boats to their berths in the inner section of the harbour. Watermouth has always been a private harbour and although a separate company, it belongs to Watermouth Castle, which lies on the land above the harbour.

Access by road

The harbour lies immediately off the A399 coast road and you will first see the signs for Watermouth Cove Holiday Park. You need to go through the entrance to this park to get to the lane that leads to the harbour. Postcode for the satnav EX34 9SJ.

Parking

Parking is available on the quay for a payment to the harbourmaster.

Water access

The round tower on Widmouth Head gives a guide into the harbour with the entrance difficult to pick out until you are almost on top of it. The entrance is easy and there are visitors' moorings just outside the inner breakwater that is covered at high water. If the tide is low it is possible to anchor just inside the entrance to await suitable water for mooring further inside but virtually all moorings dry out.

Facilities

The holiday park has a shop and café/restaurant and there is a café/restaurant at the castle and the Saw Mills pub is a 5 minute walk inland. The yacht club opens its bar on Friday and Saturday nights in the season.

More information

The harbourmaster is at ☎ 01271 865422 and there is a crane-out service and limited quantities of diesel and water are available. The yacht club can be contacted at www.watermouthyachtclub.co.uk

Comments

Watermouth Harbour is located in an idyllic spot and looking to seaward it is largely unspoilt. However, on land the holiday park and the castle, which is something of a theme park, bring you into the 21st century with a bang. They do not impinge of the harbour and this one is well worth a visit either by sea or by land. Here you get a sense of the history of this beautiful area and you can ignore the modern developments inland.

Watermouth Harbour at low tide

Combwich, River Parrett

Tucked away in the wilds of Somerset, Combwich looks as though the world has passed it by but look closely and you find that not only does it have a long history but it is very much up to date and involved in handling some critical modern cargoes. It is a small creek or pill on the banks of the River Parrett and way back there was a ferry running across the river here. In the 15th century the port was used for the export of farm produce and the import of timber and later it served for the export of bricks from the local brick yard and for the import of coal.

The creek silted up and by the 1930s it was used only by a few yachts but then a new lease of life came in the 1960s when Hinkley Point nuclear power station was built along the coast. Combwich was selected as the point for the import of the heavy

The creek at Combwich at low water

sections of the power plant for onward transport by road and a purpose built ro-ro slipway was constructed in the pill. This slipway, owned by British Energy is still in use today for the occasional heavy ro-ro cargoes headed for the West Country and it is likely to be used again when construction of the planned new nuclear power station at Hinkley Point begins.

Yachts still lie on the muddy banks of the creek and because this whole region has been inundated with floods over the years, a new raised sea defence wall around the pill offers protection but has changed the character of the pill today.

Access by road

Take the A39 out of Bridgwater and in the village of Cannington take the right turn signposted to Combwich.

Parking

There is a small parking area by the harbour and street parking.

Water access

Follow the winding channel of the River Parrett where local knowledge is advisable. There should be plenty of water from half tide onwards and it is possible to anchor in the river but contact the harbourmaster first in case any shipping is expected. Landing is possible by tender around high water but be prepared for a muddy landing.

Facilities

There is a shop and post office in the village and the Anchor Inn on the river front does food and drink The Combwich Motor and Sailing Boat Club is established in the village and offers showers.

More information

Combwich Motor and Sailing Boat Club –
www.combwichboatclub.co.uk
Harbourmaster Bridgwater –
harbourmaster@sedgemoor.gov.uk
☎ 01278 782 180

Comments

Combwich is a fascinating little harbour and it is one of the few harbours recorded in this book that still has an active and possibly expanding future. It may not be much to look at with the dominant feature being the exposed mud at low water but you can sense the history of the place and the complete absence of any of the facilities that follow the normal tourist trail give it a great feeling of a step back in history.

The new ro-ro landing facility has transformed the tiny harbour

Mud is the predominate feature of Combwich

Bridgwater, River Parrett

This wooden crane is a relic of Bridgwater's past as a port

History

Bridgwater is one of those ports that have a huge history but which has fallen a victim to road and rail transport and which has almost lost touch with the sea. The River Parrett that gives it access to the sea is still there and the banks on each side of the river in the town would be busy with shipping. The bridge across the river marked the head of navigation for sea-going vessels but cargo would be trans-shipped into sailing barges with lowering masts to continue its voyage inland. The history of Bridgwater as a port goes back to the 10th century.

During the 17th and 18th centuries Bridgwater was a busy port with mainly coal cargoes coming in and bricks and farm produce going out. It was never home to larger international trading ships because of the difficult and shallow entrance although foreign ships did come in with timber from Scandinavia. There was a regular packet ship service to Bristol.

Barges would ship cargoes inland to Langport and when the canal to Taunton was opened there was talk of having a canal right across the peninsular to Exeter to provide a means to ship the West Country mineral cargoes to South Wales avoiding the notorious Land's End route, but the full length of the canal was never completed. Trade at Bridgwater started to die out at the beginning of the 19th century although cargoes, mainly sand and building materials, still come in to Dunball Wharf about 5 miles downstream from Bridgwater.

Access by road

Bridgwater lies on the main A38 with easy access from the M5 motorway.

Parking

The best car park is the one at the Asda supermarket and there are some pay and display car parks close to the river. Dunball Wharf is further east on the A38 and has limited parking.

Sign on the bridge across the river

The abandoned waterfront at Bridgwater

Water access

It is a long and winding trip up the River Parrett from the sea and after Highbridge there are very limited facilities for yachts. It is possible to moor in Bridgwater itself at highwater and then dry out in the mud but contact the harbourmaster first.

Facilities

There is every facility you could want in Bridgwater itself and the Fountain Hotel on the quay does food and drink.

More information

Bridgwater Tourist Office at
bridgwater.tic@sedgemoor.gov.uk
Harbourmaster ✆ 01278 782 180

Comments

You can see the evidence of the past prosperity at Bridgwater in the form the elegant Georgian houses and squares, but today the town has almost turned its back on the river that was previously its lifeblood. The 18th-century bridge over the river that caused horrendous traffic jams before the motorway was built is a reminder of the history but along the river there is much modern development that takes away any sense of history, although one hand operated crane on the west quay remains. Flood defence walls have taken away some of the character of the old quays.

Uphill, Weston Bay

Mud is the predominate feature of Uphill with yachts finding a safe berth in the mud

To see Uphill today it looks like one of those impossible harbours that make you wonder why it was ever developed. Uphill goes back at least to Roman times and it is not so difficult to imagine that the hill behind the harbour would have been an attractive defensive position for a port close to the sea. Then there is the shelter from the westerly winds provided by the large mass of Brean Down and the river channel of the River Axe that wandered far inland.

This main river was an important waterway after the monks of Glastonbury reclaimed much of the surrounding marshland and Uphill, which lies up a creek off the main river channel, increased in importance when the limestone quarry at the back of the harbour was established in the 17th century. The trade at Uphill was then mainly coal coming in to feed the limekilns and lime and limestone in various forms going out. The harbour at Uphill was also used by the Severn trows that traded in the upper reaches of the Bristol Channel. The actual harbour was mainly the muddy banks of the creek with some stone hard standings.

The church on the hill dates back to the 10th century whilst the castle tower is much more recent being only 200 years old and both provide a good landmark for heading towards Uphill but they are not leading marks.

Access by road

From the A370 south of Weston-super-Mare take the turning to the hospital and then follow the road and the signs around the high ground and into the village. The boatyard and harbour are on the left at a right angle bend.

Parking

There is parking just before the entrance to the boatyard and in a section of the old quarry beyond.

The old limekiln with the limestone quarry immediately behind it

Water access

You need to be brave and have a forgiving boat to enter Uphill. The channel of the River Axe starts to the east of Brean Down and is marked by a few green and red buoys. Once in the river, the channel leading to Uphill turns off on the port side and then it is just a question of keeping on the centre line. It is soft mud all the way so grounding should not be serious provided that you are entering on the flood tide. Near the boatyard there is a serious obstruction from a sunken boat in the channel that needs careful negotiation. There may be mooring at pontoons or in the mud banks but talk to the boatyard first.

Facilities

There are two pubs and a bistro in the village as well as a shop. A beach can be found by following the road down to the sea and there is a camping site here as well.

More information

www.uphillvillage.org.uk
Uphill Boat Centre – toilets, showers and a chandlery are available. www.uphillboatcentre.co.uk

Comments

Uphill has survived many changes over the years and today at low water it can look miserable but once the harbour is flooded as the tide comes in it comes to life. The history has been preserved in the form of the limekilns and the ruined church on the hill whilst the pubs down the road give a warm welcome. The village was subject to flooding in the past but new sea defences built in the 1980's offer better protection but hide much of the harbour from view unless you climb up the banks. The best view is from the hilltop where there are superb views over the Bristol Channel to Wales.

Pontoons have been laid to provide yacht moorings but flood defences have transformed the area

Oldbury-on-Severn

Oldbury-on-Severn and its near neighbour, Littleton-upon-Severn were both small ports on the south bank of the River Severn above the road bridges that have a long history. It is thought that both inlets were used by the Romans and they provided a means of bringing cargoes to an area that was relatively remote before road transport expanded. There is rich farm land in the hinterland and Oldbury had an important brickworks that provided outbound cargoes. The two ports were mainly served by Severn trows, the flat-bottomed trading barges that would provide a link to the coal fields of South Wales as well as to many of the smaller ports along the Severn as well as to Bristol.

Both inlets suffered when the modern sea defences were built. These major works cut off much of the inlets from the sea so that today there are only moorings towards the seaward end of the creeks. Before that Littleton has an important boatyard that built many high performance racing catamarans but what was the boatyard is now an industrial estate. Oldbury is home to the Thornbury Sailing Club and they are responsible for the moorings in the creek and for a considerable area of hard-standing and the clubhouse and slipway on the eastern bank at the entrance.

The sign at the Anchor Inn points to its place in history

Access by road

From the A38 near Thornbury take the B4061 into the town and then follow the signs either to Littleton or Oldbury.

Parking

At Littleton there is parking at the end of the road by the sea wall and in Oldbury the Anchor Inn car park. Postcode for the satnav is BS35 1QA.

Only yachts use the creek that has a history going back to Roman times

The creek at Littleton where there was once a boatyard building some of the top racing multihull yachts

Water access

First you have to negotiate the channels of the Severn Estuary, passing under both Severn bridges. To get to both of these harbours you need to take the unmarked secondary channel called Oldbury Lake once the Leary Rock has been cleared. Because the channels do change local knowledge is advised. Thornbury Sailing Club has control of the moorings whilst at Littleton there is virtually nothing.

Facilities

There is a pub in the village at Littleton, the White Hart, which is over a mile from the creek. At Oldbury the Anchor Inn was also the head of navigation on the creek before the sea defences were built. Thornbury Sailing Club.

More information

www.thornburysc.org.uk

Comments

These two creeks or pills were out of the mainstream of the Severn Estuary shipping and were only used for local traffic. Today they seem even more remote as though the world has passed them by and it is only the traffic at the sailing club that shows any sign of activity. However, they are well worth a visit if only to enjoy the extensive views of the Severn Estuary and the Severn bridges and the wild remoteness of the area.